6

8

10

12

18

20

22

24

30

32

34

36

42

44

46

48

GRADUATED LOOPY BOW

1 Make a loop leaving the tail the desired length.

2 Continue making loops gradually increasing the size of the loops until the bow is full and you have enough ribbon left over to make the remaining tail.

3 Secure the center of the bow with floral wire.

4 Fan out the loops.

5 Cut the tails at an angle or in points to finish off the look of the bow.

LOOPY BOW

1 Make a loop leaving the tail the desired length.

2 Continue making loops keeping them uniform in size until the bow is full and you have enough ribbon left over to make the remaining tail.

3 Secure the center of the bow with floral wire.

4 Fan out the loops.

5 Cut the tails at an angle or in points to finish off the look of the bow.

WIRING & TAPING STEMS TOGETHER

1 Wrap a piece of floral wire around the stems.

2 Cover the wire with floral tape. The tape should be tightly wrapped around the wired stems without buckles or gaps.

FLORIST BOW

1 Measure the length of one of the ribbon tails, and with the right side of the ribbon on the outside, make a loop and squeeze the ribbon together. Hold it with your thumb and forefinger.

2 Make a full twist of the ribbon so the right side is facing out.

3 Make another loop toward the other side.

4 Make a slightly smaller set of loops on top of the first set of loops. Continue to alternate the loops, right and left, until you have made as many as you like.

5 To complete the bow, twist the remaining ribbon around your thumb to make the center loop. The remaining ribbon is the second tail. Adjust both tails so the ribbon is on the right side. Put a small piece of wire through the center of the top loop, and twist it tightly at the back of the bow to hold all the loops together. The wire should be tight enough to hold the loops, but loose enough so you can move the loops to create a full, fluffy bow.

6 Spread out the bow loops and trim the ends of the tails.

WREATH BASES

WREATH BASES

The wide variety of wreath bases can be confusing, but once you begin using the different styles, you will find that each has its' own character. Each construction lends itself to a distinctive style of wreath. Wreath bases are made from a number of materials including wire, twigs, vines, straw and styrofoam.

Wire bases are great for making Christmas wreaths. You can wire pine boughs around the frame, and hot glue ribbons and ornaments to the greenery. Twig wreaths are perfect bases for silk flowers, fruits, vegetables etc. There are many styles of twig wreaths. Flowers and leaves can be twisted onto some of the wreaths through the twigs giving a loose, informal look. Wood wrapped wreaths give a more tidy appearance and can be decorated in an orderly fashion as well as a casual, playful way.

Straw bases are very sturdy and offer good support for styrofoam anchors. Anchors can add large quantities of flowers, birdhouses, etc. to the inside or outside of a base. Attach an anchor by wiring a piece of styrofoam to the base with 24 gauge wire.

Styrofoam bases are perfect for making elegant wreaths out of dried flora as well as silk flowers. A low melt glue gun is the perfect tool for securing your materials to the wreath.

Wreaths are easy and satisfying to make. Even the most elaborate wreaths are actually very

Vine wreath

Twig wreath

Wood wrapped wreath

Straw base wreath

easy to put together. By leaving a wreath base partially exposed, it can become an integral part of the wreaths' design adding an open airy look.

You can use some of the bases over and over. The vine, twig, wire, and wood wrapped wreaths are very forgiving. If you aren't happy with your wreath, pull the material off and start over. If you are tired of the wreath you made last year, make a new one using the same base.

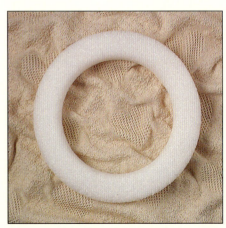
Styrofoam base wreath

Twig frame

Grapevine arch

APPLICATION

Most materials can be secured to wreaths in five ways:

Hot glue gun or glue pot
  To secure materials to natural wreaths like twig, vine, wood and straw

Low melt glue gun
  To secure materials to styrofoam

Tacky white glue
  To secure materials to styrofoam (hot glue can melt styrofoam)

Florist wire
  To secure materials to twiggy wreath bases that do not have a solid gluing surface

Ribbons
  To secure objects and materials to all bases

Sometimes it's difficult to know where to begin when designing a wreath. Here are eight basic layout ideas to help.

1 Cover wreath evenly with flowers. A bow is not always necessary.

2 Begin with a bow placed at the bottom center and arrange the flowers to flow in a downward arch.

3 Arrange flowers so that the upper left and lower right are a mirror image.

4 Begin with a bow placed in the upper left, and build the arrangement flowing to the upper right and lower left.

5 Center a bow on the bottom of the wreath and build flowers up each side, leaving the top open.

6 Place a bow in the upper right side, arrange flowers around 1/2 of the right side and around 1/4 of the left side.

7 Start with a bow on the upper left side and arrange flowers off the wreath instead of following the contour.

8 Affix a bow to the top center and arrange flowers in a backward "S" shape. Follow the shape and extend beyond the wreath.

SPRING WREATH HAT

Materials

- 1-17" (Yellow) straw sun hat
- 3 (2 X 1") Floral foam squares
- 4 Stems (yellow) daffodils
- 4 Stems (lavender) tulips
- 4 Stems (Purple) freesia sprays X 3
- 5 Stems (Pink) lilac sprays X 2

Tools

- Glue gun/glue sticks
- Wire cutters

1 Hot glue the 3 squares of foam to the left side of the hat as close to the crown as possible.

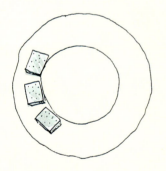

Instructions

2 Cut two daffodil stems to 5", and insert one in the first piece of foam with the flower pointing upwards. Place the second one in the second piece of foam with the flower facing upward and outward. Cut the third daffodil stem to 3" and insert in the third piece of foam facing straight out. Cut the last daffodil stem to 9" and insert in the third foam facing downward.

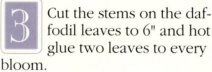

3 Cut the stems on the daffodil leaves to 6" and hot glue two leaves to every bloom.

4 Cut the leaves from the tulips and set them aside. Cut three tulip stems to 2", and cut one tulip stem to 6" Add to the foam following the same pattern as the daffodils.

5 Hot glue one tulip leaf behind each tulip. Hot glue one extra leaf over the longest tulip stem.

6 Cut each freesia spray into 3 smaller stems and insert in foam as shown.

7 Cut each lilac stem to 3" (10 stems). Hot glue blooms in-between all the other flowers filling in any empty spaces and covering the foam.

SUMMERS' DREAM WREATH

Materials

- 🌸 1-18" Floral foam wreath
- 🌸 Spaghnum moss
- 🌸 50 Floral pins
- 🌸 1 (Variegated) large spider plant with babies
- 🌸 5 Stems (orange) oriental poppies
- 🌸 3 Stems (blue) agapanthus
- 🌸 7 Stems (purple) liatris
- 🌸 10 Stems (yellow) tiger lilies
- 🌸 6 Stems (purple) azalea sprays X3

Tools

- 🌸 Wire cutters
- 🌸 Low melt glue gun/glue sticks

Instructions:

1 Cover the front and sides of the wreath with moss. Secure the moss with floral pins.

2 Bend the stem of the spider plant sideways and push it into the wreath. Bend the leaves of the spider plant upwards and downwards making the plant mostly flat. Let the "baby" plants hang naturally.

3 Cut 2 poppy stems to 8", and insert one above the spider plant, following the bend of the wreath and one below the spider plant. (Suggestion: glue stem tips before inserting into foam.) Cut remaining three poppy stems to 6", and add one to the center of the spider plant and the rest on the opposite side of the wreath alternating the buds and open blooms. Distribute them evenly spaced.

4 Cut the agapantha stems to 3", and insert in foam around wreath equally spaced.

5 Cut the liatris stems to 2", and add to the outside of the wreath keeping the blooms facing the same direction. Place the liatris every 8" or so, and keep them evenly spaced.

6 Cut the lily stems to 4", and add in-between flowers, filling in empty spaces.

7 Cut each azalea stem into three, 10" pieces. Insert each spray of flowers into the wreath at an angle. Fill in any remaining empty spaces.

Pretty Pansy Wreath

Materials

- 1-6" Grapevine wreath
- 2 Stems (purple) pansy sprays
- 4 Stems (yellow) dry look roses X3

Tools

- Glue gun/glue sticks
- Wire cutters

Instructions:

1 Remove all the pansy blooms and buds from the sprays. Set the leaves aside. Hot glue the backs of the open blooms as you place them next to each other, one inch apart around the front of the wreath. Hot glue the buds in-between the open blooms.

2 Remove the leaves from the pansy sprays, and hot glue two leaves facing out, in opposite directions under each pansy.

3 Remove the roses from the stems (twelve blooms), and hot glue the roses (on top of the leaves) all around the wreath in-between the pansies.

BRIDAL FANTASY WREATH

Materials

- 1-16" (White) twig wreath
- 5 Yds. (white) 2" wired ribbon
- 12 Stems (cream) open garden roses
- 1 (Variegated) small ivy bush (14 stems)
- 5 Stems (white) babys' breath sprays
- 12 Stems (red) dry look rose buds
- Floral wire

Tools

- Glue gun/glue sticks
- Wire cutters

1 Using three yards of the ribbon, hot glue one end to the twigs at the top, center of the wreath. Loop the ribbon back and forth around the wreath, tucking it under the twigs between the loops. When you are back to the starting point, secure the end with hot glue.

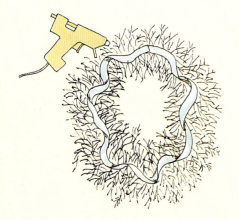

2 With the remaining ribbon make a seven inch wide, 8 loop, graduated loopy bow with 4" tails (see page 2). Hot glue the bow onto the wreath where the two ends of the looped ribbon meet.

3 Pull the open roses from the stems, and hot glue them all around the wreath next to the ribbon. Alternate the roses back and forth over the ribbon keeping them at least three inches apart.

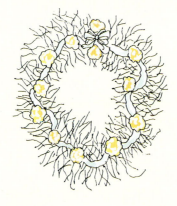

4 Hot glue two sets of rose leaves under each rose. Alternate the directions of the leaves.

5 Cut the ivy bush into single stems (14). Hot glue three small pieces to the outside of the bow. Beginning on the right side of the bow, add the rest of the ivy around the wreath. Alternate the pieces back and forth over the ribbon.

6 Remove each cluster of flowers from the babys' breath, and hot glue each cluster one inch apart around the wreath. Face some inward and some outward from the ribbon.

7 Cut the rose bud stems to 4", and hot glue to the wreath every six inches. Alternate the roses back and forth across the ribbon.

Muted Flower Garland

Materials

- 2 Yds. (dark green) paper ribbon
- 5 Stems (blue) hydrangeas
- 10 Stems (mauve) magnolia X 2
- 6 Stems (cream) mini babys' breath X3
- 3 Floral wires

Tools

- Glue gun/glue sticks
- Wire cutters
- Scissors

Instructions:

1 Unfold the paper ribbon and cut a four inch wide, six foot long strip.

2 Place an 18" piece of wire around the ribbon every 18". Fold the wire in half, and wrap the ends around the ribbon three times. Bend the twisted wire into a small loop.

3 After the wires are in place, lay the ribbon flat on a table to add the flowers. Cut each hydrangea into clusters of three flowers. Using half of the clusters, hot glue one cluster to the right of the center wire facing right. Place one cluster to the left of the center wire facing left. Continue gluing clusters down the ribbon to the right and left every two inches. As you glue the clusters, alternate from side to side along the ribbon.

4 Hot glue the remaining hydrangea clusters down the ribbon the same way except place each cluster facing opposite the first set.

5 Remove the flowers from the magnolia stems (20 blooms). Hot glue one large bloom over the center wire. Place the remaining flowers on either side of the large bloom. Alternate the flowers from side to side in-between the hydrangeas.

6 Cut clusters of flowers from the babys' breath stems. Distribute them evenly along the ribbon in-between the flowers. Hot glue to secure.

Note: You can either hang the garland on the wall from the small wire loops, shape it into a wreath or drape it over a screen or a piece of furniture. The garland is very flexible and can be folded into almost any desired shape.

JUICY FRUIT WREATH

Materials

- 1-10" Styrofoam wreath
- 12 oz (Natural) excelsior (wood fibers)
- 50 Floral pins
- 4 (Yellow) large pears
- 6 (Red) large apples
- 3 Large oranges
- 2 Large peaches
- 2 Stems (gold) black eyed susans
- 4 Stems (blue) dry look statice
- 1 (Purple) large grape cluster

Tools

- Low melt glue gun/glue sticks
- Wire cutters

Instructions:

1 Cover the front and sides of the wreath with excelsior. Secure the excelsior with the floral pins.

2 Place a large amount of glue on the back side of each pear as you place one at the top and one on the bottom in the center of the wreath. Place the other two at three and nine o'clock.

3 Glue the bottom of each of the apples as you place one to the left of each pear and the remaining two on the inside of the wreath next to the side pears.

4 Glue the oranges on the bottom as you place them next to the apples. Keep them evenly spaced on the wreath.

5 Glue the peaches on the bottom as you place one at the top of the wreath between the apple and the pear and the other on the inside center of the wreath.

6 Cut the black eyed susan stems to 3" and distribute them evenly around the wreath in-between the fruit. (Save the leaves.)

7 Cut the statice stems to 1", and glue to wreath following the same pattern as the black eyed susans.

8 Glue the black eyed susan leaves around the flowers.

9 Cut the grapes from the cluster, and glue each grape to the wreath alternating the sizes and distributing them evenly spaced.

Indoor Trellis

Materials:

- 17" Twig wreath
- 1 Small (green) ivy spray
- 3 Stems (pink) natural sweet peas
- 6 Stems large (mauve) colonial hydrangeas
- 7 Stems (wine) floribunda roses
- 8 Stems (cream) wild roses X4

Tools

- Hot glue gun/glue sticks
- Wire cutters

Instructions:

1 Cut ivy spray into single pieces. Secure ivy by twisting the ends around or under twigs on the wreath. Hot glue if necessary.

2 Cut the sweet peas just below the bottom leaf and place them at equal distances around the wreath. Bend the flowers in opposite directions, and wind each one through the twigs so they stay securely in place.

3 Cut the hydrangeas just above the third leaf and add to wreath by bending the stems through the twigs. Place hydrangeas in center of each sweet pea and in-between each sweet pea.

4 Cut roses just above the second leaf and distribute them evenly around the wreath. Bend the stems through the twigs to secure.

5 Cut the wild roses below the lowest bloom and add to wreath using the same method as above. Spread them evenly and heavily throughout.

PINK MAGNOLIA SWAG

Materials

- *Floral foam (6 X 3 X 3")*
- *Sphagnum moss*
- *Floral pins*
- *10 (Gold) bamboo sticks*
- *3 Stems (mauve) large, latex magnolias*
- *Floral wire*

Tools

- *Serrated knife*
- *Hot glue gun/glue sticks*

Instructions:

1 Cover front and sides of floral foam with moss. Secure the moss with floral pins.

2 Remove all the leaves from the magnolia stems, and set them aside.

3 Cut the first magnolia 6" below the bloom and place in the upper center section of the foam. Cut the second magnolia stem to 4", and add to the center of the foam. Cut the last magnolia stem to 8", and add to the bottom of the foam. (Hot glue stem tips before inserting into foam.)

4 The magnolia leaves should have a three inch wire. If they don't, hot glue a 3" piece of floral wire onto each one. Insert three leaves facing upwards around the top magnolia. Place five leaves around the center magnolia with two facing upwards, one to the side and two facing downward. Place two leaves around the bottom magnolia with one of them below the bloom.

5 Add the bamboo. Use 11" branches for the top of the arrangement and 18" branches for the bottom. Stagger the heights of the center branches, and insert them in the foam facing both upwards and downwards.

Summer Sunflower Swag

Materials

- 1 Floral foam (7 X 3")
- Spaghnum moss
- Floral pins
- 9 Stems (blue) dried look larkspur
- 4 Stems (gold) medium sunflowers
- 25 (Natural) raffia strands
- 2 Stems (orange) aster sprays X3
- 4 Stems (light yellow) September flower sprays X3

Tools

- Wire cutters
- Glue gun/glue sticks

Instructions:

1 Cover front and sides of floral foam with moss. Secure the moss with floral pins.

2 Cut two larkspur stems to 5" and insert one in each side of the foam. (Hot glue stem tips before inserting into foam.) Cut two larkspur stems to 3" and insert horizontally in the top of the foam so they overlap the first two stems. Cut four larkspur stems to 12" and insert the ends horizontally in the top of the foam (in the center) with the tips facing outward in opposite directions. Set aside the remaining larkspur.

3 Cut the leaves from the sunflowers. Set aside. Cut two sunflower stems to 6" long, and insert one into each side of the floral foam in-between the larkspur. Cut the other two sunflower stems to 4", and add to the center front of the foam.

4 Hot glue one sunflower leaf to the bottom of each sunflower. Point the leaves towards the larkspur.

5 Tie a knot in the center of the raffia. Secure the raffia knot to the center of the foam with a floral pin. Wind the raffia through the flowers in both directions. Loop the ends over the longest larkspur a few times, then let the excess raffia hang free.

6 Cut each aster spray into three, single, 6-8" stems. Place one stem near each of the outside sunflowers and the rest in the middle of the swag.

7 Cut the September flowers into single stems and fill in throughout the swag following the same pattern as the larkspur.

8 Cut the last piece of larkspur into 6" pieces and fill the center of the swag.

Easter Lily Swag

Materials

- 3 Stems (white) Easter lily sprays X2
- 5 Stems (yellow) delphinium
- 3 Stems (pink) phlox
- 4 Yards (floral print) 1-1/2" wired cotton ribbon
- Floral tape
- Floral wire

Tools

- Wire cutters
- Scissors

Instructions

1 Lay the lilies on a table. Stagger the lengths until they measure one yard long.

2 Add the delphinium to the lilies. Stagger the heights, placing one taller than the lilies, one just below the first one in the center and three off to the sides. Cut the stems even with the lily stems. Wire the stems together eight inches from the bottom of the stems, and cover with floral tape. (See page 2.)

3 Place one phlox in the center near the tallest lily. Place the other two lower and off to the sides. Tape the phlox to the other stems.

4 Using three yards of the ribbon, make a nine inch wide, 12 loop graduated loopy bow without tails. (See page 2.) Set aside.

5 Wrap the remaining ribbon around the stems and tie a knot. Wind the tails in and out of the flowers.

6 Wire the bow to the knot.

7 Make a hanging loop on the back of the tied ribbon. Hang the swag with the bow on top and the flowers downward or lay the swag on a table.

26

Spring Wisteria Swag

Materials

- *12 X 4 X 2" Floral foam*
- *Spaghnum moss*
- *Floral pins*
- *3 Stems (lavender) wisteria*
- *5 Stems (lavender) morning glories*
- *3 Yds. (green/lavender) 2" wired ribbon*
- *1 (Magenta) tulip bush X14*
- *5 Stems (terra cotta) rununcula sprays X2*
- *Floral wire*

Tools

- *Wire cutters*
- *Glue gun/glue sticks*
- *Serrated knife*

Instructions

1 Cover front and sides of floral foam with moss. Secure the moss with floral pins.

2 Cut the wisteria into single stems. Place one stem on either end of the foam. Place two stems on top center facing opposite directions and two stems in center front facing opposite directions. Place two more stems in center front next to the last two, and place the last stem in center bottom. (Hot glue stem tips before inserting into foam.)

3 Hot glue extra wisteria leaves around the base of each bloom.

4 Insert one morning glory on each side of the swag and two closer to the center; with one stem facing up and one down. Cut the last stem into sections, and fill in the center with flowers facing upwards and downwards.

5 Make a nine inch wide, 10 loop graduated loopy bow with 4" tails and hot glue to center of swag. (See page 2.)

6 Cut tulip bush into single stems (14), and distribute in an even pattern.

7 Cut rununculas into single stems, and distribute throughout swag filling in empty spaces.

Jurassic Wreath

Materials

- 1-16" (white) open grapevine wreath
- 3-9" long (Primary colored) dinosaurs
- 5 Stems (red) gerbera daisies
- 3 Stems (navy blue) mini carnations X3
- 1 Stem (natural) black eyed susan X4
- 2 Stems (purple) wild flower sprays X3
- 4 Stems (pink) mini pansies X3
- Floral wire

Tools

- Glue gun/glue sticks
- Wire cutters

Instructions:

1 Wire the dinosaurs to the wreath equally spaced.

2 Cut the gerbera stems to 2", and hot glue around wreath equally spaced.

3 Cut the carnation stems to 2" and hot glue in-between the gerberas.

4 Cut the black eyed susan stems to 2", (save the leaves) and hot glue to wreath. See photo.

5 Cut the wild flower sprays into 3 single stems each, then cut each single stem in two. Add to wreath like the other flowers keeping them evenly spaced and filling in blank areas.

6 Cut pansy stems to 2", and hot glue to wreath in empty areas next to the blue carnations.

7 Hot glue the black eyed susan leaves around the wreath under the flowers.

30

BABY SHOWER WREATH

Materials

- 1-16" (White) double grapevine wreath
- 6 (Miscellaneous) baby items
- 5 Yds. (pink) 1/4" satin ribbon
- 5 Yds. (blue) 1/4" satin ribbon
- 3 Stems (pink) babys' breath X3
- 3 Stems (blue) babys' breath X3

Tools

- Wire cutters
- Scissors

Instructions

1 Cut a 24" strip of blue and pink ribbon. Cut the remaining ribbons into 12" strips.

2 Using the 24" strips, for the larger items, tie the duck and the bottle on the wreath. Tie each of the baby items on the wreath with the remaining strips. Tie the ribbon tails into simple bows.

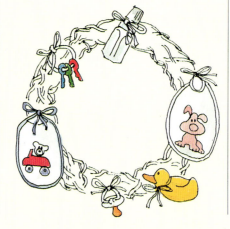

3 Cut the babys' breath sprays into single stems (nine stems for each color).

4 Make six bunches of flowers from the single stems. Place three stems in each bunch alternating two blue with one pink or two pink with one blue. Tie each of the bunches onto the wreath, in-between the baby items, with the remaining strips of ribbon. Bend the stems of the flowers slightly so they follow the curve of the wreath.

THE GARDENERS' WREATH

Materials

- 1-18" Styrofoam wreath
- 12 oz (Natural) excelsior
- 50 Floral pins
- 5-2" (Terra cotta) plant pots
- 5 Pkgs. (herb) seeds
- 5 (Herb) garden markers
- 3 Stems (gold) large sunflowers
- 5 Stems (purple) gerbera daisies
- 3 Stems (orange) azara sprays X3
- 38 Single stems (yellow and burgundy) dry straw flowers
- 6 Stems (purple) dry statice
- Floral wire

Tools

- Low melt glue gun/glue sticks
- Wire cutters

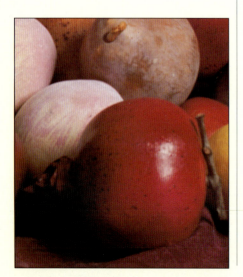

Instructions

1 Cover the front and sides of the wreath with excelsior. Secure the excelsior with floral pins.

2 Run an 18" floral wire through the hole in the bottom of the plant pots. Twist the ends of the wire together behind the pot and push the wire into the wreath. Place the pots evenly spaced with 6" to 8" between each pot.

3 Glue one seed package inside of each plant pot.

4 Glue one garden marker into each plant pot.

5 Cut the sunflower stems to 2", and hot glue them in-between the flower pots. Glue three sunflower leaves around each bloom. (See photo.)

6 Cut the gerbera stems to 2", and insert two stems into the wreath between the pots where there are no sunflowers. Place the extra gerbera on the other side of the wreath between two sunflowers to balance the colors.

7 Cut the azara stems apart so that each flower cluster is single with a 2" wire stem. Insert the clusters every four inches or so around the wreath.

8 Cut off the straw flower stems, and glue the blooms all around the wreath every three inches or so.

9 Cut the statice stems to 2", and fill in empty spaces between the flowers. Glue to secure.

Sweetheart Wreath

Materials

- 1-6" Heart shape, styrofoam wreath
- Spaghnum moss
- Floral pins
- 6 Stems (red) dry look rose bud sprays X7 (or 42 dried baby rose buds)
- 4 Yds. (rose) 1/4" double satin ribbon
- 1 Stem (white) babys' breath
- Floral wire

Tools

- Wire cutters
- Low melt glue gun/glue sticks
- Scissors

Instructions

1 Cover the top and sides of the wreath with moss. Secure the moss with floral pins.

2 Cut roses from spray leaving 1" stems. Glue one rose every inch along the top center of the wreath. Glue one rose every 1-1/2" along the outside of the wreath. Place the outside roses in-between the top roses. Place a row of roses along the inside of the wreath opposite the outside buds. Cluster two roses at the top where the heart meets and two roses at the bottom point.

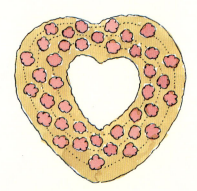

3 Make ribbon loops across the front of the wreath using two yards of ribbon. Dab some glue on the end of the ribbon, and place the ribbon at the top where the heart meets. Then, loop the ribbon up and down all over the wreath. Glue the ribbon down wherever it touches the wreath.

4 Make a five inch wide, loopy bow with the remaining 2 yards of ribbon. (See page 2.) Glue it to the center of the wreath.

5 Break the blossoms from the babys' breath and glue each one to the wreath in-between the rose-buds.

FALL FLOWERS AND FRUIT

Materials

- 1-14" (Natural) willow wreath
- 2 Yds. (plaid) 2" cotton ribbon
- 15 Strands (natural) raffia
- 1 (Brown and gold) fall leaf bush (6 stems)
- 5 Stems (yellow) small sunflowers
- 5 Stems (dark blue) grape clusters
- 3 Stems (orange) zinnias
- Floral wire

Tools

- Scissors
- Glue gun/glue sticks

Instructions

1 Cut one yard of the ribbon, and hot glue onto wreath.

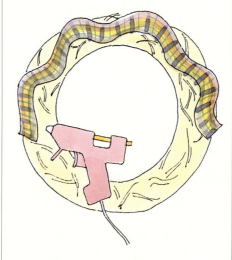

2 Make a seven inch wide, 4 loop florist bow with 4" tails with the remaining ribbon (see page 3). Hot glue the bow to the wreath as shown in the photo.

3 Tie a knot in the center of the raffia strands to bind them together. Hot glue the knot behind the bow and drape the tails around the wreath on either side of the bow.

4 Cut the leaves from the stems on the fall bush and hot glue clusters of three all around the wreath. Hot glue a few extra leaves around the bow.

5 Cut the sunflower stems to 2", and hot glue one or two flowers over each leaf cluster and around the bow.

6 Hot glue the grapes to the wreath placing two on either side of the bow and the other three evenly spaced around the lower part of the wreath. Bend the grapes to follow the shape of the wreath.

7 Cut the zinnia stems to 2", and hot glue to wreath as shown in the photo.

8 Fill in any blank areas with fall leaves.

Golden Fall Swag

Materials

- 1 Block of floral foam
- Sphagnum moss
- Floral pins
- 3 Yds.(metallic, floral print) 2" wired ribbon
- 5 Stems (gold) birch
- 1 Stem (brown) fall leaf
- 8 Stems (red) dry look roses
- 6 Stems (yellow) ranunculas
- 2 Stems (yellow) sunflowers X2
- Floral wire

Tools

- Wire cutters
- Scissors
- Glue gun/glue sticks

Instructions

1 Cover the front and sides of the foam with moss. Secure the moss with floral pins.

2 Cut 2 birch stems to 1-1/2", and place one draping out the left side and the other draping out the right side. Cut two stems to 8" and place one in top center of foam and one in bottom center of foam. Cut the remaining stems to various lengths between 1-4". Staggering the placement, fill in the foam with the sticks pointing outward in both directions from the center.

3 Cut the fall leaf stem into single 4" pieces. Hot glue them to the moss (and birch branches) throughout the swag. Keep the leaves facing the same direction as the branches.

4 Make an eight inch wide, 8 loop florist bow using two yards of ribbon (see page 3). Hot glue to the center of the swag.

5 Cut the remaining ribbon in half. Beginning under the bow, hot glue the tails straight out in opposite directions.

6 Cut two rose stems to 12", and insert one out the left end and one out the right end. Cut two more rose stems to 4", and insert them above and below the bow. Cut two roses to 6" and two to 2".

Insert on the sides of the bow, keeping the shorter roses closer to the bow and the longer ones closer to the ends of the swag.

7 Add the ranunculas the same way you added the roses keeping them in-between the roses.

8 Cut the sunflowers into single 4" stems. Place them all around the bow towards the center of the swag.

9 Use remaining leaves from roses and ranun-culas to fill in any empty spots.

Happy Halloween Swag

(See page 2.)

Materials

- 1 Floral foam (2 X 12")
- Floral moss
- Floral pins
- 3 Stems (fall) leaves
- 3 Yds. (black) 1/2" satin ribbon
- 14 (Orange) paper pumpkins (assorted sizes, 1-3")
- 1 Pkg. (small) fake spider web
- Floral wire

Tools

- Wire cutters
- Serrated knife
- Glue gun/glue sticks
- Scissorsents

Instructions

1 Cover the front and sides of the foam with moss. Secure the moss with floral pins.

2 Remove the fall leaves from the stems. Hot glue one leaf down the center. Add the rest of the leaves facing out from the center in both directions.

3 Cut one yard of ribbon. Lay it over the top of the swag so the length is even on both sides of the center. Hot glue the ribbon to the center. Loop the ribbon up and down and side to side on either side of the swag. Secure the ribbon with hot glue wherever it touches the moss.

4 Make a four inch wide, loopy bow without tails with the remaining ribbon. (See page 2.) Hot glue to top of swag.

5 Hot glue the bottom of the pumpkins as you place the largest one in the center of the bow; the medium pumpkins on each side of the bow and the tiny pumpkins evenly spaced across the swag.

6 Stretch the fake spider web out in your hand, and add small clusters across the top of the swag. Fill in any empty spaces, and place some over the pumpkins and leaves.

Note: Use the Halloween swag as a centerpiece, on your door or anywhere else in your home to create the spirit of the Halloween holiday.

HOLIDAY SWAG

Materials

- 1-3' Silk pine garland
- 5 Yds. (metallic gold) 2" wired ribbon
- 5-4" (gold) pine cones
- 8-1" (clear) ornament balls
- Floral wire

Tools

- Glue gun/glue sticks
- Scissors
- Wire cutters

Instructions

If a 3' pine garland can't be found, cut a 3' piece off a larger garland.

1 Cut a three yard piece of ribbon and make an eight inch wide,10 loop florist bow without tails. (See page 3.) Hot glue or wire the bow to the top of the garland leaving a few pine stems above the bow.

2 Fold the remaining ribbon in two making two "tails", with one tail much longer than the other. Hot glue or wire the tails under the bow, and loop the tails through the swag in and out of the pine needles.

3 Hot glue or wire the pine cones to the swag. Place the first one just under the bow. Leave about 3-4" before adding the next one. Change the directions of the pinecones as you add them to the rest of the swag.

4 Hot glue or wire the clear balls onto the swag. Place two above the bow and one just below the bow. Place the other five in-between the pinecones changing sides the way you placed the pinecones.

Materials

- 1-9' Christmas garland
- 5 Yds. (red) 2" wired velvet ribbon
- 10 Stems (red) single poinsettias
- 3 Stems (gold) cedar branches
- 4 Stems (Variegated) holly with berries
- 9 (Natural) large pinecones
- Floral wire

Tools

- Glue gun/glue sticks
- Wire cutters
- Scissors

Instructions

1 Hot glue the end of the ribbon to the end of the garland. Weave the ribbon back and forth along the "top" of the garland creating loops or puffs along the way. Secure the ribbon to the garland every foot with a dab of hot glue.

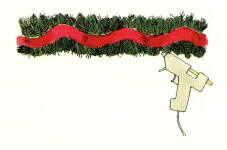

2 Cut flowers and leaves from poinsettia stems. Glue one bloom every 8-10" along the garland. Hot glue two leaves under each bloom.

3 Cut the leaves from the cedar branch, and hot glue them onto the garland around and in-between the poinsettias.

4 Cut the holly stems into small clusters, and hot glue them in-between the poinsettias.

5 Hot glue the bottom of the pinecones as you place them in-between the poinsettias.

Note: Hot glue is the quickest method of adding everything to the garland, but each piece may also be individually wired with #20 gauge florist wire and wired onto the garland base.

Yuletide Wreath

Materials

- 1-18" Styrofoam wreath
- Spaghnum moss
- 50 Floral pins
- 6 (Natural) Douglas fir branches
- 2-1/2 Yds. (red) 2" velvet wired ribbon
- 2 Stems (gold) pine branches
- 7 Stems (red) medium poinsettias
- 4 Stems (green) holly with berries
- 6 Stems (red) dry look roses
- 5 (Burgundy) berry clusters
- 35 (Gold) prickled maple berries (or "liquid amber")
- Floral wire

Tools

- Wire cutters
- Scissors
- Low melt glue gun/glue sticks

Instructions

1 Cover the front and sides of the wreath with moss. Secure the moss with floral pins.

2 Cut the Douglas fir branches into single stems. Glue each piece onto wreath one inch apart. Cover the wreath as heavily as possible.

3 Cut 1-1/2 yards of ribbon and make a seven inch wide, 7 loop, graduated loopy bow (see page 2). Set aside. Glue the remaining yard of ribbon all around wreath until the end reaches the starting point. Glue the bow over the ribbon where the ribbon meets at the top.

4 Cut the leaves off the gold pine stems, and glue them onto the wreath. Distribute them evenly, turning the leaves to face different directions.

5 Cut poinsettia stems to 1", and glue two on either side of the bow. Glue two more lower on the sides of the wreath and glue one in the bottom center section.

6 Cut holly stems to 1", and glue clusters throughout wreath in the same style as the gold pine.

7 Cut rose stems to 1", and glue flowers around the wreath every 8-10".

8 Cut each berry cluster into three sections, and glue each section to wreath every five inches.

9 Glue each prickle ball (or liquid amber ball) to wreath 2-3" apart filling in any empty spaces..